WORLD IN VIEW

FRANCE

Cate Milner

STECK-VAUGHN
L I B R A R Y
Austin, Texas

Published in the United States in 1990 by Steck-Vaughn Co., Austin, Texas, a subsidiary of National Education Corporation

© Macmillan Publishers Limited 1989

First published 1989

Published by Macmillan Children's Books
A division of MACMILLAN PUBLISHERS LTD

Designed by Julian Holland Publishing Ltd
Picture research by Jennifer Johnson

Library of Congress Cataloging-in-Publication Data

Milner, Cate, 1961-
    France/Cate Milner.
      .p. cm.—(World in view)
    Summary: Surveys the people, geography, history, economy, way of life, and industry of France.
      ISBN 0-8114-2427-8
      1. France—Juvenile literature. [1. France.] I. Title.   89-21783
    DC17.M54 1990   CIP
    944—dc20   AC

Printed and bound in the United States
1 2 3 4 5 6 7 8 9 0 LB 94 93 92 91 90

Photographic Credits
Cover: Barnaby's Picture Library, title page: J. Allan Cash, 7 J. Allan Cash, 8 Picturepoint, 11 Bruce Coleman Ltd. 12 Judyth Platt, 15 Helen Rogers/Trip, 17 J. Allan Cash, 19 Picturepoint, 21/24/26 J. Alan Cash, 29 Sheridan Photo Library (Ancient Art & Architecture Collection), 31, J. Allan Cash, 33 Bridgeman Art Library, 35 Mansell Collection, 37 Helene Rogers/Trip, 40 Mary Evans Picture Library, 42 Bridgeman Art Library, 45/46 Hulton Picture Co., 48 Topham, 49 Helene Rogers/Trip, 51 Robert Harding Photograph Library, 53 Picturepoint, 54 Helene Rogers/Trip, 57 Renault Ltd., 58/59/61/63 J. Allan Cash, 65 Picturepoint, 67 Science Photo Library, 69 J. Allan Cash, 72 Picturepoint, 72 Helene Rogers/Trip, 75 Picturepoint, 81 Mark Antman/Topham, 83 Tony Staples, 84 James Davis Worldwide Photographic, 86/69 J. Allan Cash, 92 Allsport (Vandystadt), 93 Helene Rogers/Trip.

Contents

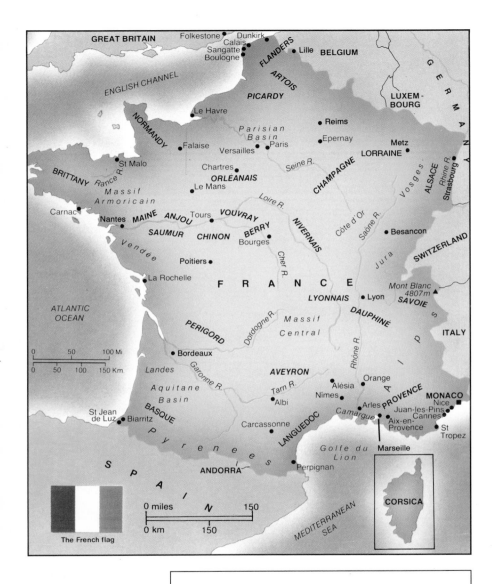

The French flag is called the *Tricolor* because it has three blocks of color: blue, white, and red. The design was in use before the French Revolution. The blue and red are the colors of the city of Paris and the white was a symbol of royalty.

4

1   Introduction

France is situated in the heart of Europe and is sometimes called "the hexagon" because of its shape. This important central position has made it a melting pot of culture, trade, race, knowledge, and language. France is a country of contrasts and surprises.

It is the largest country in Western Europe and covers about 211,200 square miles. This includes the Mediterranean island of Corsica, which is part of France. France is twice as big as Great Britain, but 17 times smaller than the United States and 14 times smaller than Australia. The country stretches about 625 miles from north to south and almost the same distance from east to west.

Four different seas lap the French coastline. To the extreme north is the North Sea with its busy traffic of fishing boats and tankers. The narrow channel of sea along the Normandy and Brittany coastline is called the English Channel in Britain, but in France it is called La Manche, which means The Sleeve. The remainder of the west coast is bordered by the Atlantic Ocean, and the southeast coast is on the warm, tideless Mediterranean Sea.

The borders of France
France's frontiers stretch for 3,440 miles and 40 percent of them separate France from its many neighbors. Those neighbors are Belgium, Luxembourg, Germany, Switzerland, Italy, Monaco, Spain, and Andorra. The mountain chains of the Alps in the east and the Pyrenees in the southwest

FRANCE

The unit of currency in France is the franc. The franc was first introduced in the 1300s, but was used as the basic unit of a decimal system after 1795. This system divided the franc into 100 centimes. Many countries have now adopted this decimal system for their currency including Italy, Greece, and Great Britain. The centime, franc, five francs, and ten francs are issued as coins. The larger sums are usually paper notes, of which the largest is F500.

form natural barriers, but even these obstacles to transportation have passes through them. France has therefore never been completely cut off from any of the neighboring countries with which it shares a border.

Physical geography

France can be roughly divided into four main geographical areas. To the north and west is the main agricultural region, where there are plains and plateaus with fertile soil and a climate that is good for growing crops. The largest group of plains is known as the Paris Basin, which consists of a number of plateaus and hills that slope down to the low-lying Paris-Orléans region.

To the south and east there are narrow valleys and high hills rising to spectacular mountains in the Alps and the Jura. Mont Blanc, the highest

In contrast to the rolling plains of the north, the southwest border of France is very mountainous. This photograph shows Mont Blanc, the highest mountain in Europe. It marks the border between France and Italy. A road tunnel of 7.5 miles runs through the mountain to link the two countries. The tunnel opened in 1962.

peak in Europe at just over 15,600 feet, is in the Alps.

The largest geographical region in France is the Massif Central, a mountainous area covering about one sixth of the whole of the country. In the north and northwest it gradually merges with the plains. To the southeast however it has sharp high mountains that overlook the Languedoc region and the plains around the Rhône River and the Saône River. The delta of the Rhône River is known as the Camargue Region.

In the southwest the mountain range of the Pyrenees, forming the 280-mile border with Spain, shelters the Basque region in its foothills.

Climate
France has a mild climate with four noticeable seasons. The average temperature for the year is not less than 50°F in the north and only exceeds 58°F near the Mediterranean Sea. The total annual rainfall is rarely less than 19.5 inches.

To the north of the Loire River the weather is more changeable, cooler, and with more rain than to the south. Farther south, in Provence, near the Mediterranean, summers are very dry. The weather there is hotter than in any other part of France. It rains for less than 100 days a year and is the most popular tourist region of France.

The south of France is affected by three winds. The "mistral," which is a cold, violent wind that blows from the north down the Rhône Valley, the "tramontana" that blows from the northeast across the Alps, and the strong southeasterly wind, the "marin," that blows inland from the Mediterranean.

The fortress of Polignac was built on the basalt core of an extinct volcano. The whole area around Polignac and the nearby town of Le Puy is covered with small volcanic hills, called puys, *rocky outcrops, and craters that are the remains of ancient volcanoes. There are also hot springs. Several rivers, including the Loire, rise in this region.*

Plant life

France's flora is greatly varied. The climate is favorable to vegetation and long ago much of the country was covered in forests. To the north the land is cultivated and open fields dominate the landscape. In the Paris Basin, grain crops are grown and some forests still exist, such as Rambouillet and Fontainebleau. In Brittany, to the west, different kinds of landscapes are to be found, such as woodland, pastures, and moorland with heather, gorse bushes, and broom.

9

In the Mediterranean area vines, olive trees, cork trees, box trees, thyme, rosemary, and green oak forest all grow well in the dry climate. Some plants have adapted by developing long roots and others have water reservoirs. Orange and lemon trees are grown near Nice, and rice is grown in the flat lands of the Camargue.

There are two types of vegetation distinctive to the south of France. The first is the *maquis*. This is a growth of bushes, small trees, and short leathery plants, closely intertwined and very difficult to penetrate. (The *maquis* was also the name given to the French Resistance army during World War II.) The second kind is the *garrigue*, similar to the *maquis* but less overgrown, with many evergreen shrubs. Both kinds of vegetation are found on poor land.

In the Alps, the vegetation changes as the altitude gets higher. On the lower slopes there are forests of deciduous trees that lose their leaves with the onset of winter. Higher up, evergreen pine forests grow below mountain pastures. On the banks of the Loire, the Rhine, and the Garonne Rivers are the vines that have made France famous for good wines.

Wildlife

There are more than 90 species of mammals, 400 birds, 25 amphibians, and 27 reptiles in France. Being part of mainland Europe, France shares much of its fauna with other countries. Long ago, bison, lynx, wild cats, wild boar, and red deer used to inhabit the forests that covered most of the country. Wild cats, wild boar, and red deer have survived but they are rare. Some animals are especially worthy of note. Chamois, ibex, and marmots can be found in the Alps and bears can still be found in the Pyrenees. The Pyrenees also provide shelter for a special kind of muskrat found only in France. Many animals, including beavers, and all birds of prey, are protected by law in France.

The Camargue is inhabited by herons, egrets, and wild horses. It is the only place in Europe where flamingoes nest, and the biggest lagoon in that region is a bird sanctuary. There are over 100 nature reserves in France altogether. The western coast provides an ideal habitat for thousands of birds. Many migrating birds from Northern Europe rest on French soil for a while before going on to Africa, and other migrant birds spend their winters in France.

These flamingoes are in the Camargue which is an area of marshy land formed by the delta of the Rhône River. The Camargue covers about 215 square miles and is famous for its wildlife. It is one of the biggest areas of marshland in Europe. Black bulls, bred for the bull ring, and half-wild horses roam across it.

The Seine River carries a lot of heavy traffic as it twists its way to the sea. These barges at Rouen carry coal, grain, and other goods to and from the port at Le Havre. Barge families live on the barges and take their cars with them, so they can use their cars in the places they visit.

The rivers

The main rivers in France are the Rhône, the Seine, the Loire, and the Garonne. The Loire is the longest river in France, measuring 634 miles. Today, it is too shallow to be sailed on, but once it was an important waterway. It has a rich heritage of great houses, or châteaux, which draws visitors from far and wide. Some of the greatest vineyards in France line its banks.

The Seine is only 485 miles long, and it flows through Paris, the capital. Unlike the Loire, it is a busy river, carrying boats and barges up and down stream.

The Rhône is the largest river in the southeast. However, it rises in Switzerland and only 324 miles of its 505 miles is in France. Its waters swell when the snow and glaciers melt in the spring, and also during heavy rainfall. Nowadays, the Rhône River is used for hydroelectric plants, irrigation, and the cooling of nuclear power plants.

The Garonne is the shortest of the main French rivers, measuring 360 miles. With its source high in the Pyrenees, its floods are unpredictable and dangerous in winter, because of heavy rainfall, and in spring, when the snow melts. One of its tributaries is the Dordogne, which is famous for the wine that is produced on its banks near Bordeaux. This part of the country is very popular with tourists.

Population

There are just over 55 million people living in France. This is slightly less than the population of Britain, but more than three times greater than that of Australia. The United States on the other hand has a population four times larger than France. Compared with Great Britain, however, France's population has more room to breathe, because Britain has more than three times the number of people per square mile.

The most heavily populated cities and their suburbs are Paris, with nine million inhabitants, followed by Marseille and Lyon with just over one million each.

2 Paris and the Regions of France

The regions of France are very different from one another. Each has its own identity with its own specialities, its own type of industry or agriculture, and its own kind of scenery.

Paris, city of light

The capital of France is Paris, in the north of the country, on the banks of the Seine River. Sometimes called the "city of light," Paris has been admired and loved by millions for centuries and has inspired writers and artists alike.

The government, the banks, the stock exchange, and the head offices of many big firms are based in Paris, making it the political, economic, and financial capital of France. The city is a crossroads for road, air, and rail traffic, and also an important center of communications.

The Paris region is an industrial center as well. The main industries in the area are steel, iron, and cars, but chemical, food, and electronic industries are based here, too. There is a very large work force in and around Paris. Nine million people live in the area, although only just over two million live in the city itself. Five million people commute to work on the underground subway, or *Métro*, every day.

To meet the increasing housing demands, new towns such as Sarcelles have been built outside Paris. In the older small towns on the outskirts, large apartment buildings have been built, changing the atmosphere and character of the town. Paris is now the world's sixth largest metropolitan area.

Lastly, Paris is world renowned as a cultural and intellectual center, and the city's museums and palaces house many artistic masterpieces.

Some places of interest

Paris received its name from a tribe of Celtic fishermen called the Parisii, who settled on an island in the middle of the Seine River in the third century B.C. The island is now called the Ile de la Cité and lies in the center of the capital.

After the Romans invaded the area, they occupied the south bank of the Seine River by the island. Roman ruins such as baths, arenas, theaters, and a forum have survived there. Today, this part of

This photograph of Paris is taken from the Eiffel Tower. The buildings and gardens of the Palais de Chaillot are fine examples of the elegant architecture for which Paris is famous. In the distance are the trees of the Bois de Boulogne and the skyscrapers of the new commercial districts to the west of the city.

Paris is called the Latin Quarter.

It was not until the reign of King Clovis in A.D. 508 that Paris became a capital. For a long time, the city was surrounded by boundary walls, which grew as Paris itself grew. Over the ages, buildings and monuments were erected to form what is now one of the world's most beautiful cities. Landmarks were erected such as the Cathedral of Notre Dame, completed in 1345. The Sorbonne University, founded in 1253, is one of Europe's oldest universities. Kings and queens built palaces in the city, such as the Louvre, the Tuileries, and the Luxembourg Palace. The Louvre was changed to a museum in 1793, and is one of the largest and most famous museums in the world.

Much later, in the nineteenth century, Baron Haussman transformed many parts of old Paris with daring urban planning. He demolished whole areas in order to create *grands boulevards*, such as the Boulevard des Capucines, and open areas like the Place de l'Opéra. He also completed the Place de l'Etoile in which the Arc de Triomphe stands. The Arc de Triomphe, built to commemorate Napoleon Bonaparte's victories, was completed in 1836. In 1920, the grave of an unknown soldier was put there. A perpetual flame burns at the grave to commemorate the dead of the two World Wars.

The Eiffel Tower, perhaps the most famous Parisian landmark of all, was built for the Great Exhibition of 1889 by Gustave Eiffel. Originally 984 feet high, today it is 1,052 feet high, since a television antenna has been added. It is now used for telecommunication purposes, as well as welcoming tourists to observe the city from its heights.

France has always been at the forefront of new ideas in art and design and the Pompidou Center is an example of the recent ideas in design. The center houses a museum of modern art and an exhibition center. It was named after Georges Pompidou, the President of France from 1969-74, who was very interested in encouraging new ideas.

Many parts of Paris have been redeveloped in recent years. Les Halles used to be the main food market in Paris. In the 1970s the market was moved out of Paris. On the site where the market was located a modern construction of metal and glass was built, housing shops, a museum, exhibitions, cafés, restaurants, and cinemas. The atmosphere is young and lively and Les Halles is now a very fashionable part of town.

The Pompidou Center in the Beaubourg area is one of the more popular buildings in Paris, with

seven million people visiting it each year. It houses a vast public library and a modern art musuem as well as an important exhibition hall. The area around the center is a hive of activity. Jugglers, fire-eaters, painters, fortune tellers, acrobats, and mime artists, as well as the street cafés, all contribute to a colorful street life where people are happy to stroll.

The Musée d'Orsay opened in 1986. Originally a train station, the building has been completely renovated. It has exhibits that cover all aspects of art from 1848 to 1914, and includes many famous impressionist paintings as well as furniture and other artifacts of the period.

Flanders, Artois, and Picardy
In the extreme north of the country near Belgium are the regions known as Flanders, Artois, and Picardy. There the countryside is flat, often only broken by the slag heaps of the large coal-mining industry in the area. Northern France has seen much fighting over the centuries. Battles in the Middle Ages and during both World Wars I and II took place in northern France. Some of the trenches from World War I have been preserved, and many monuments and cemeteries are to be found commemorating those who gave their lives there.

Dunkirk, Calais, and Boulogne are the main ports of the region, and their principal trade is fishing. Boulogne and Calais, however, are also important ferry ports from which boats leave for Britain at frequent intervals. In 1993, the Euro-tunnel is expected to emerge at Sangatte near Calais from Shakespeare Cliff near Folkestone in Britain.

This Normandy farmhouse shows many of the traditional features of the buildings of the area. The half-timbered walls and the overhanging thatched roof are seen all over Normandy. This way of building with timbers and straw is called colombage. *Behind the cottage is a château or manor house. The style of these varies all over the country, but there is usually at least one to be found in every village.*

Normandy

Normandy is in northwest France, and is well known for its cider and its apple brandy, called Calvados, as well as for its butter and cheese. In general, the food in Normandy is very rich. Typical Norman countryside has small green fields, cows, apple trees, and half-timbered black and white cottages. The region got its name when Norse raiders from Scandinavia eventually settled in Normandy.

One famous Norman was William the Conqueror, who invaded Britain in 1066 and became king there. He came from the town of

Falaise. Normandy was the scene of the 1944 D-Day beach landings on June 6 by the Allied armies, who went on to liberate France from German occupation during World War II.

The Ile de France and Champagne

The Ile de France is the region around Paris. It is called "the island of France," because this was once the whole of France. At that time it was surrounded by the lands of many lords and barons, and only through a series of marriages, alliances, and wars did France become what it is today.

The Ile de France is full of historic buildings such as the châteaux of Versailles, Chantilly, Fontainebleau, and Rambouillet. The region has many forests and is excellent for growing crops, since it has fertile soil and a mild climate.

Champagne is the region east of Paris, best known for the sparkling wine produced near Epernay. Only wines made in vineyards within a certain area in the region are allowed to be called champagne.

Alsace and Lorraine

Alsace and Lorraine form an important industrial region in the east of France along the German border. The land is fertile and there are valuable deposits of minerals such as iron ore and potassium. The area has been part of Germany as well as of France during its checkered past, being finally returned to France after World War I in 1918. Strasbourg, one of the main towns in the area, is the seat of the Council of Europe, which promotes European unity and protects human rights.

Brittany

Brittany is the region on the western peninsula of France. Its northern coastline is broken by cliffs and rocks, whereas the southern coast is flatter with long sandy beaches. Brittany was first settled by the ancient Celts in the far distant past. Breton people speak a Celtic language similar to that spoken by Welsh and Cornish people, who are also Celts. Regional specialities include butter and cider as well as other agricultural produce, and fishing is an important industry.

Ancient monuments dating back to the earliest inhabitants of France are to be found in Brittany. Large boulders called menhirs are scattered around the countryside. Dolmens, thought to be ancient tombs, are also a feature of the region. Perhaps the most amazing monument of all is at Carnac, where there are prehistoric stones standing in row after row. These may be connected with ancient burials in the area, but no one knows for certain why they were erected.

The château of Chenonceaux is built on the Cher River, which is a tributary of the Loire. Built between 1515 and 1578, it is a fine example of Renaissance architecture. The long gallery is actually built across the Cher.

The regions along the Loire River

The Loire is a wide slow river that crosses many regions, including Lyonnais, Bourgogne, Nivernais, Berry, Orléanais, and Anjou. The region most visited by tourists is probably the one where the châteaux of the Loire can be found. This area was popular with royalty and magnificent châteaux, such as Chambord, Blois, and Chenonceaux, were built by kings and queens.

Many regions along the Loire produce wines such as Saumur, Anjou, Vouvray, Chinon, and Sauvignon. Famous towns include Tours, the chief tourist center for the Loire valley, and Orléans, once the second city in France after Paris. Bourges has a beautiful cathedral and also claims to be at the center of France. Chartres has perhaps the most well known cathedral. Its beautiful, thirteenth-century stained-glass windows are world famous. Le Mans, in Maine, another area of the Loire, is renowned for the 24-hour car race held there every year.

Bourgogne and Lyonnais

The most striking feature of the Loire regions is the vineyards of the Côte d'Or which means "Golden Slopes." These vineyards produce the famous burgundy wines. Chablis and Mâcon wines are also produced in the area.

The town of Dijon is best known for the yellow mustard it exports all over the world. Lyon is located where the Rhône and Sâone rivers join, and is now the second largest city in France. It has a university and is a lively cultural and economic center. Lyon is also an important place for food, due to its many gourmet restaurants.

Franche-Comté

Franche-Comté is in eastern France below Alsace and Lorraine, and there the forest-covered Jura mountains are to be found. Comté is the local cheese and the town of Besançon is noted for its watchmakers.

Poitou-Charentes

Poitou-Charentes is in western France between the Loire and the Garonne Rivers. Part of the area is called the Vendée. This is along the coast below Brittany. During the French Revolution the people from the Vendée revolted against the new government, which ruled by executing anyone who opposed it. They were called the "Chouans" after the sound of their rallying call. The Vendée is now popular with vacationers. The region has a number of historical towns. La Rochelle is a fortified port, and Poitiers is the site of a fourth-century baptistery and a famous old church, Notre-Dame-la-Grande.

Limousin, Marche, Auvergne, and Bourbonnais

These regions are in the Massif Central, a geographical area of extinct volcanoes in central France. Auvergne has a number of interesting old towns and churches built in the twelfth century and even earlier, and Limousin is famous for fine china, enamel, and Aubusson tapestries.

Savoie and Dauphiné

Savoie and Dauphiné are in eastern France near the Swiss and Italian borders. The French Alps are in these regions, making the area very popular in the winter for skiing.

The Tarn River has cut a deep gorge through the mountains of the Massif Central. Rocky cliffs are typical of the area and provide a habitat for a great variety of plant and wildlife, including Europe's only vultures. The area was the most isolated part of France until quite recently, when new roads were built.

Guyenne, Gascogne, and the Basque region

These regions cover southwestern France, and include the Dordogne River which threads its way through the hills. Tourists enjoy the countryside around the Dordogne since the weather there is usually good and the small towns and villages are historically interesting. The Lascaux caves with their prehistoric paintings are another remarkable feature in the Dordogne.

Farther south there are the pine forests of the Landes. Near the Spanish border, Biarritz and St.

Jean de Luz are famous seaside resorts where people can go surfing.

The Basque region is on the Spanish border in the western Pyrenees. The Basques have their own culture as well as their own language. Basque people are well known as sheep raisers and for the game of pelota. Pelota is played by two teams on a court with a wall, called a *fronton*, at one end. A player from each team has to catch the ball as it bounces off the wall and try to return it. Players wear a long wicker glove called a *chistera*.

Languedoc Roussillon

The Languedoc Roussillon province is on the west Mediterranean coast. One famous sight there is the Pont du Gard, a three-tiered aqueduct. It was built by the Romans to divert the Eure River to the Roman town of Nîmes. The aqueduct is no longer used to divert water, but it still serves as a bridge.

Carcassonne is a medieval fortified town complete with watch towers and battlements. Other historic towns include Montpellier, Toulouse, Albi, and Perpignan. Much of France's table wine comes from this region.

The name Languedoc comes from *langue d'oc* meaning the "oc" language which used to be spoken in southern regions of France. "Oc" meant "yes," whereas the language spoken in northern parts of France used "öil" for "yes." The word Languedoc now, however, simply means one particular area in southern France.

Provence

Provence is hot and dry in summer and is a favorite place for summer vacations. Retired

25

The south of France is famous for its beaches and excellent weather. People from all over Europe come to places such as Cannes, on the Côte d'Azur, for their vacations. Many of the places are very fashionable and many famous and wealthy people have homes there. Cannes is also famous for its film festival, which is held every year.

people often go there to live, especially to the Mediterranean seaside resorts such as Nice, Cannes, Juan-les-Pins, or St. Tropez. Some of the world's most famous perfumes are manufactured in Grasse. Sheep rearing, olive growing, and wine making are other important industries in the region. There are numerous Roman remains to be found in Provence, particularly in the towns of Orange, Arles, and Aix-en-Provence.

The Camargue is the part of Provence where the Rhône flows into the Mediterranean. Rice grows on its marshlands and mounted herdsmen look after the wild cattle and white horses that roam free.

Corsica

Corsica is an island off the southern coast of France which became part of France in 1769. Napoleon Bonaparte, who became Emperor of France, was born on Corsica, in Ajaccio. The Corsican countryside is quite unspoiled and much of it is covered by the closely intertwined, leathery evergreen shrubs and small trees of *maquis*.

The overseas territories

France also has a number of overseas territories and countries, called *départements*, that are not separate countries but are considered to be part of France. These regions are called *Départments d'Outre Mer* and *Territoires d'Outre Mer* or overseas countries and territories. The DOM TOM as they are called, include the islands of La Réunion, Martinique, and Guadeloupe, French Polynesia, French Guyana, and others. Each separate *département*, whether in mainland France or abroad, sends a deputy to the French parliament.

3   France's Early History

The first signs of human life in France are flint tools dating back 100,000 years. Beautiful paintings and drawings in the Lascaux and the Pêche Merle caves in the Dordogne and Périgord region are other traces of early human life in France. The earliest paintings, from 30,000 years ago, show animals such as bison, horses, deer, bears, mammoth, ibex, ponies, rhinos, cows, and many more. The artists used natural coloring such as ochre and carbon to make the browns, reds, blacks, and yellows of their paintings, which are mainly of animals and hunting scenes. There are few pictures of humans.

The standing stones of Carnac

Later traces of early inhabitants are the remains of burial mounds. Stones were grouped together to form a burial chamber and then covered in earth and menhirs, or standing stones. The biggest and most impressive concentration of stones is at Carnac in Brittany. Three thousand menhir are lined up in parallel rows sometimes stretching as far as 3 miles. No one yet knows why the stones were set up in this way, although there are many theories.

Early humans in France led a nomadic life, moving from place to place according to the seasons and the food supply. They were hunters and food gatherers, and probably moved around in groups of 20 to 25 people.

They lived in shelters, sometimes in the open air, sometimes under cliff overhangs, or in caves.

In the area known as the Dordogne there are many caves in which early people lived. These wall paintings are over 20,000 years old. They can be seen in the cave at Pech-Merle, which was discovered in 1922. The artists have drawn images of the horses found in the area at that time. They have even signed the paintings by making handprints!

There are remains of these settlements in the Dordogne and other regions. Gradually, the early humans developed. They started to farm the land, trade any extra food they might grow, and learned how to work metal.

Gaul and the Gauls

The first known prehistoric tribes in Europe were the Celts. They lived in an area that the Romans called Gaul. Gaul included what is today France, Belgium, western Germany, and northern Italy. The people of Gaul were not nomads as the early inhabitants of France had been, but instead preferred to settle in groups. They were farmers, hunters, craftspeople, musicians, storytellers or bards, and some were miners.

The Gaul's food was simple, consisting mainly of bread and boiled or roasted meat. They drank beer brewed from barley, and some drank wine. Their clothes were brightly colored and made of linen and wool.

The Druid was the most important man in the community. Druids were a mixture of priest, teacher, and judge. They performed sacrifices, taught the tribal chief's children, passed judgment, and took care of the sacred oak groves. The Gaul's religion involved worship of the spirits of the forests and nature. The Gauls were a cultured people. They valued music and the spoken word and created their own artistic style, decorating their jewelry and buildings with geometric, animal, and floral designs.

When the Romans began to expand their empire, Julius Caesar launched a campaign to conquer Gaul. The Gauls fought back, and in 53 B.C. Vercingetorix, one of the Gallic chiefs, led an attack against the Roman army. This revolt ended with the siege of Alésia in the Auvergne by the Romans. The town surrendered and Vercingetorix had to lay down his weapons at Caesar's feet. By 50 B.C. Julius Caesar's army had conquered Gaul right up to the western bank of the Rhine River.

Gaul under the Romans

As part of the Roman empire, Gaul grew in many ways. It developed trade with other parts of the empire, providing food such as grain, olive oil, and wine as well as woolen cloth, bronze, glassware, and iron from its mines. In the first century A.D. the country became one of the richest regions in the whole of the empire.

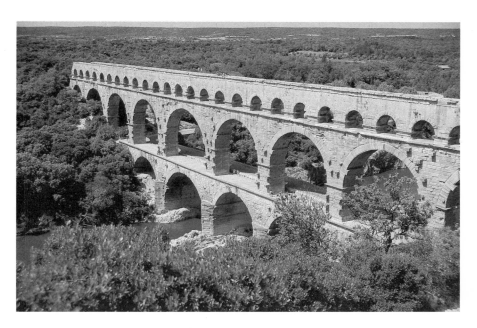

The Pont-du Gard was built by the Romans in 19 B.C. to carry water across the Gard River to Nîmes in the south of France. It is about 900 feet long and 160 feet high. The upper portion was an aqueduct and the lower part carries a road, which is still in use.

Gaul's heritage from the Romans includes masterpieces such as the Pont du Gard aqueduct near Nîmes, the theater at Orange, and the amphitheater at Arles.

From the third century the Roman empire began to weaken and decline. In the fifth century, the region of Gaul broke the last ties with its Roman conquerors.

Merovingian Gaul

Visigoths, Franks, Alamani, and Burgundians each invaded and occupied Gaul in the fourth and fifth centuries. Most important of these were the Franks, from whom France got its name. They originally came from a region near the lower part of the Rhine River, and had invaded and settled in one area, now called Belgium. The Frank's leader,

31

Clovis, wanted to conquer all of Gaul. In the second century, Christianity had been introduced into Gaul and the country was now a Christian center. Clovis said that he would become a Christian if God helped him to victory in his battles against the Alamani. The Franks were victorious and Clovis and 3,000 of his warriors were baptized by the Bishop of Reims.

Clovis succeeded in establishing the most powerful Christian kingdom of his time, reigning until his death in 511. The Merovingian dynasty of kings, named after Clovis's grandfather, Merovech, lost their power. Later Merovingian kings became known as the "Lazy Kings," or *Rois Fainéants*.

The Carolingian kings
Eventually the Merovingians were succeeded by the Carolingian dynasty, and the first of these kings was Pepin II in 687.

The most famous Carolingian king was Charlemagne. He came to the throne in 771 and was later crowned Emperor of the Romans. During his reign, Charlemagne extended the boundaries of his country until at last his realm spread from western France into today's Germany, and from the Pyrenees and northern Italy in the south to Denmark in the north. After Charlemagne's death, the empire he had built was split up and divided among his three sons. Naturally, it lost the strong position it had once held.

During the eighth and ninth centuries and part of the tenth century, France was often attacked by her neighbors. From Spain and Africa in the south came the Muslims, and from Scandinavia in the north came the Vikings. In the eighth century African Muslims invaded Carolingian France. Charles Martel, or Charles the Hammer, was able to stop their advance at Tours and force them back over the Pyrenees into Spain.

The Vikings looted, plundered, and pillaged the countryside along the coast, and took over the area now called Normandy. Charles the Simple later gave this land to the Vikings, and it became the Duchy of Normandy. It was from here in 1066 that William the Conqueror invaded Britain.

The Capetian dynasty

The Capetian dynasty succeeded the Carolingian kings. At the beginning, the Capetian kings were not powerful rulers and some of the surrounding

This fifteenth century manuscript shows Joan of Arc being tied to a stake before being burned to death in 1431. After helping Charles VII to become king she was captured by the Burgundians who sold her to the English. They accused her of heresy. She was made a saint in 1920.

33

lands had more power than the king. As time passed, however, the Capetians grew more influential.

The best-known and most-loved Capetian king was Louis IX who became Saint Louis. He came to the throne in 1226 and tried hard to govern France in a just manner. He was very religious and went on two crusades to recapture the Holy Land. He died in 1270.

Joan of Arc

1337 saw the start of the Hundred Years' War between England and France. The English kings believed they had some claim to the French throne, and at first they had many victories. The course of the war was changed, however, by a young girl named Joan of Arc.

The daughter of a peasant family, Joan of Arc was born in 1412 at Domrémy in northeastern France. During her childhood she is said to have heard voices asking her to save France. Joan's voices told her to go to Orléans, where the English were besieging the town. She was to end the siege and then take the future King Charles VII to Reims to be crowned. Joan amazed everyone by doing exactly this. She dressed in men's clothing and armor and rode at the head of the army. Her courage was an inspiration and the French army won battle after battle. Finally, Joan was taken prisoner by the Burgundians and sold to the English. She was tried for witchcraft and found guilty. The king did nothing to save her, and she was burned at the stake in Rouen on May 30, 1431, at the age of 19. By 1453 the Hundred Years' War was over and the only piece of France that England had left was Calais. Joan of Arc is now France's patron saint.

The Bourbon dynasty

Louis XIV had the most glittering court in sixteenth-century Europe. Vast sums of money were spent on entertainments, such as this feast held in the courtyard of his palace. The huge marble fountain has been decorated with hundreds of candles to make a column of light. The feast was attended by the most important of the 2,000 courtiers who lived in the palace.

In the sixteenth century, France was divided by religious wars. Catholics and Protestants, called Huguenots, were at loggerheads. After much bloodshed, Henri de Navarre was able to unite the country. Although he was a Huguenot, he became a Catholic in order to be crowned Henri IV, the first Bourbon King of France. Henri IV drew up the Edict of Nantes in 1598, giving the Huguenots freedom to worship in certain areas of the country. Henri IV was a tolerant and popular king. In 1610, however, he was assassinated and Louis XIII took his place. The new king was too young to reign and his mother, Marie de Medici, took over as regent. Later, Louis XIII had a very astute adviser in Cardinal Richelieu. Richelieu became prime minister, and by his policies helped to make France strong.

35

The Sun King

Louis XIV succeeded Louis XIII in 1643 at the age of five. He grew up to be one of the most flamboyant kings of France, calling himself the "Sun King." As a child in Paris, Louis XIV experienced the civil uprisings of the *Fronde*, when some of the nobles were fighting the government. He always hated Paris as a result. So, on some marshland to the west of Paris where his father had had a shooting lodge, Louis XIV built the amazing Palace of Versailles. He moved the whole court and the ministers there, and kept them occupied with balls, plays, music, and intrigues. This gave the nobles no time to plot against him. His plan was so successful that Louis XIV reigned for 68 years. When at last he died in 1715, he left France crippled with the debts of his extravagant court life and costly wars.

4　The Revolution of 1789

The Revolution of 1789

On the eve of the French Revolution, France was governed by Louis XVI, who had been king since 1774. France had been a monarchy for over ten centuries. Louis XVI had absolute power, which meant that he did not need to consult a parliament or senate before making a decision or passing a law. For instance, Louis XVI could send a person to prison without trial just by sending a letter to him or her. These were called *lettres de cachet*.

The people in 1789

The people of France could be roughly split into three groups. There were the nobles, the clergy, and the rest. Neither the nobility nor the Church

The Palace of Versailles was built between 1676 and 1708 on the site of a royal hunting lodge. The palace includes the great château and two smaller ones, the Grand Trianon and the Petit Trianon, which was a favorite of Queen Marie Antoniette. The palace is set in extensive grounds with statues, lakes, and woodland.

had much to complain about. Both received taxes from the peasants but paid few taxes to the king. Both were powerful. The nobility owned 20 to 25 percent of the land, which was a source of riches.

The rest of the nation was made up of the *bourgeois* and the peasants. The *bourgeois* made up a fairly new section of the population. Although not having the privileges of the nobility and the Church, they were not poor like the peasants. Many had become wealthy through their trade, while others were artisans, teachers, and so on.

Versailles

Louis XVI lived at Versailles, the enormous palace built by his ancestor Louis XIV. Versailles was very beautiful. It had many big rooms with painted ceilings, full of rich carpets, gilded furniture, and priceless masterpieces.

The most famous room in the palace was the Hall of Mirrors, a long room with large French windows on one side. Mirrors covered all the other walls and, in Louis XVI's time, the hall was full of solid silver furniture right down to the flower pots! It must have been a magical sight in the evenings, when the candlelight from the chandeliers reflected in the mirrors and the furniture.

Around the palace there were huge gardens, including a large lake, many fountains, theaters, and ballrooms. There was even a mock village created for Marie Antoinette, Louis XVI's queen. All this cost an enormous amount of money. In fact, over 10 percent of the state's total income went toward the upkeep of the king and his court. Versailles can still be visited today, although much of the furniture has been sold.

The people with most grounds for discontent were the peasants. They represented 80 percent of the population but had no rights at all. They were crippled by the taxes that they paid to the king, to the Church, and to the local lord. In all, between 30 and 60 percent of the peasants' income was spent on taxes.

To add to their misery, the crops in 1788 had been poor. The winter had been so cold that the Seine River had frozen from Paris to Rouen. This meant that food was in short supply. It has been estimated that on the eve of the French Revolution one-fifth of the population had no resources at all.

A national assembly

It was in this atmosphere of discontent that a national assembly was called. Every section of the population was represented by delegates from all over France. On June 20, 1789, the delegates representing the peasants and the bourgeois took an oath to give France a constitution. This is a written document that lays out how a government will be run, what it believes in, and the laws it will follow. This famous oath was taken in the royal Real Tennis courts, because Louis XVI had ordered that the room where the delegates usually met should be locked. It is known, therefore, as the oath of the *Jeu de Paume*, which means "real tennis."

Storming the Bastille

Meanwhile Parisians were closely following all the events at the assembly. Thousands of hungry people thronged the streets, and their mood was ugly. At last, being afraid for life and property, a

The fortress prison of the Bastille was built in about 1370 as part of the protective walls around Paris. In the 1700s, it was seen as a symbol of the corrupt Bourbon monarchy. On July 14, 1789, the Bastille was stormed and captured. In spite of the fact there were only seven prisoners to be freed, this was seen as the start of the French Revolution.

crowd of citizens went to the prison of the Bastille, where arms and ammunition were kept, to ask for weapons to defend themselves. On being refused, they attacked and quickly captured the prison. The taking of the Bastille was seen as a symbol of royal power crumbling under the will of the people. It happened on July 14, 1789, and marks the beginning of the Revolution. France still celebrates this day and it is a national holiday.

Soon after, the assembly decided to establish a constitutional monarchy. This meant that the king had little power left, and the assembly now had the power to make laws.

A crowd of people came to get the king and his family from Versailles to take them back to the capital. The Parisians called the royal family *Le Boulanger, La Boulangère, et le petit mitron* or the Baker, the Bakeress, and their apprentice. This was because the king and his family were believed to be able to provide the nation with the food it so badly needed.

From then on, differences of opinion began to emerge among the members of the assembly who had once been united in their wish to change France. Various parties developed, such as the Jacobins, the Feuillants, the Cordeliers, the Girondins, the Montagnards, and the *Sans Culottes*, so called because they wore trousers not knee-length leggings.

The king is executed
The political atmosphere gradually became more and more explosive. Desperate, Louis XVI tried to escape over the northern frontier with his family. However, he was caught and brought back to Paris. By now the people no longer trusted him, and he was imprisoned. On January 21, 1793, he was beheaded. Later that year, on October 16, his wife Marie Antoinette was also beheaded.

New governments rapidly succeeded one another to power. Each was more extreme than the last, ending with a dictatorship run by the Revolutionary Government. A revolutionary calendar was created and the date went back to year one. Churches were closed. Instead of worshiping a Christian god, people were encouraged to worship the goddess of reason and intelligence. Children were no longer given Christian names of saints but were called names such as Freedom or Constitution.

From March 1793 until July 1794, in what was called the Reign of Terror, nobody felt safe. Anybody at all could be accused of being anti-revolutionary or a traitor, and sent to the guillotine. It is estimated that in that year, between 35,000 and 40,000 were victims of the terror.

Napoleon Bonaparte

The dictatorship was eventually overthrown. A more moderate government took its place, called the *Directoire* government, and a man who was to change the face of France began his rise to power. That man was Napoleon Bonaparte.

The paintings by Jacques Louis David is of Napoleon crossing the Alps. It shows him as leader of the army. His campaigns to conquer Europe cost France a great deal of money. In 1813, his attempt to capture Russia met with disaster. Half a million of his soldiers died and he lost much of his popularity. Although he tried to regain his power, he was finally exiled to the island of St. Helena.

Bonaparte was born in 1769 in Corsica. He was a brilliant military strategist and had become a brigadier general at the early age of 24. He led many successful campaigns in Italy, Austria, and Egypt. In 1799 he became First Consul of the French Republic, and in 1804 he crowned himself Emperor Napoleon I.

Napoleon's ambition was boundless, and at one time his empire dominated Europe. Then his luck changed, and in 1812 he failed in his attempt to conquer Russia. A year later, he was defeated by a joint European army. Napoleon was forced to abdicate in 1814, and was briefly exiled to the island of Elba. He returned to France only to be defeated again at Waterloo in 1815. He was exiled once more, this time to the island of St. Helena. He died there in 1821.

Many things that Napoleon did still exist today. He created the national bank or Banque de France. He established the high school system or the *lycées*. He also had the code of law drawn up, called the *Code Civil*.

After Napoleon's reign, the monarchy was restored with first Louis XVIII and then Charles X. France had gone full circle. Social inequalities still existed, with peasants and workers leading very poor, humble lives.

5 Into the Twentieth Century

France at the turn of the century was a country full of changes. Many exciting achievements were being made. The Eiffel Tower, a masterpiece of engineering, had been completed in 1889. The Impressionist painters, such as Claude Monet and Edgar Degas, were experimenting with new painting techniques. Louis Pasteur had recently discovered how to prevent certain diseases by vaccination. The Lumière brothers had developed a cinematograph to make moving pictures, and in 1895 they made their first film. In 1898, Marie and Pierre Curie discovered radium, now widely used to treat certain illnesses. Then, at the start of the twentieth century, in 1909, Louis Blériot flew across the English Channel from Calais to Dover for the first time. The world was shrinking because of the better transportation available. It was a time of great optimism.

World War I

The shadow that came to change everything was World War I. The war broke out in August 1914, setting France, Russia, Britain, Belgium, and Serbia at war with Germany and the Austro-Hungarian Empire. France felt well-armed and confident, and everyone assumed that the war would be over in a few months.

Instead of months, the war lasted for four years. Eventually, Germany and her allies agreed to sign an armistice on November 11, 1918. The armistice

During the first two years of World War I the fighting took place in Belgium and northern France. Large areas of land were totally devastated, with shell craters, and mud churned up by the tanks, as far as the eye could see. In the summer, after the battles, the ground was covered in poppies which grow in disturbed soil. This is why the Flanders poppy is worn to remember the war dead.

is still commemorated to this day, when wreaths are laid on war memorials all over France.

The death toll had been larger than in any previous war. France had lost 1.4 million men and in all of Europe over 8.5 million soldiers had been killed and millions injured. People said it was the war to end all wars.

World War II

Only twenty years later, however, France was plunged into another war with Germany. This time it was not fully prepared, and on June 22, 1940, France was forced to sign an agreement with Germany. By 1942 France was totally occupied by the Nazi army.

Living in France under the German occupation was hard. Food was rationed and there was little

During World War II, France was occupied by the German army. During the Occupation life in France was very difficult for most French people. Once again many towns and villages were damaged, especially in the north, as the Allied armies drove the Germans out of France.

or nothing to spare. Jews were persecuted, and thousands were sent off to concentration camps in Germany, to be exterminated in the gas chambers or to work at forced labor.

Some French people collaborated with the Germans. Others left France to answer General de Gaulle's call to arms. He was setting up the army of the "Free French" in Britain. Still other

French people joined the secret Resistance movement, known as the *maquis*. This was a very courageous step to take. The *maquisards*, as they were called, tried by various means to hamper the enemy's movements. The Resistance destroyed many strategic points such as ammunition dumps, railroad lines, bridges, and trains.

The Resistance helped the British and the Allies in other ways. They sheltered airmen who had been shot down by the Germans, and helped them over the Spanish border so that they could get back to Britain.

Eventually, in the summer of 1944, France was freed by British, American, Free French Army, and other Allied troops, and the occupation was over. France lost fewer lives than in World War I. In all, 620,000 French people were killed. Of these, 200,000 were soldiers, 160,000 were civilians, and 240,000 had died in German prison camps.

Looking forward

After World War II, France adopted a new attitude of optimism and of faith in the future. Many of France's factories, railroad structures, and buildings had been damaged, if not destroyed, in the war. Towns and ports, especially in the north, had been flattened. For example, nearly the entire town of Falaise was destroyed. This eventually turned out to be an advantage, since France was able to build new railroads and factories that were more efficient and up-to-date. Farms and shops were modernized too, and France gradually rebuilt its economy. In 1957, France joined the European Economic Community, or the EEC, which made trade easier between the member countries.

Electing the government

In September 1958, General de Gaulle, who was now president, held a referendum on France's constitution and, as a result, the present structure of the French government and parliament was created. The president is the head of the government and is elected by the people for seven years. Once elected, the president chooses his prime minister and other ministers from the party with the majority in parliament. The prime minister, president, and other ministers have to put the laws into effect. The president himself can decide laws, hold referenda, and negotiate with other nations.

The parliament is made up of two chambers, the National Assembly and the Senate, which together have legislative power. The National Assembly is elected every five years by national election, and can be dissolved by the president. The Senate is elected for nine years but all members do not stand for election at the same time. Senators are elected by deputies and local councilors.

During 1968, there were demonstrations against government policies and particularly against the overcrowded conditions in the universities. These students are surrounded by the French riot police. Although everything is peaceful here, violent riots broke out later.

Other major events since World War II include the Algerian War of Independence. Algeria had been a French colony, but in 1962 President Charles de Gaulle granted Algeria's independence. Since the Algerian war there has been an influx of North African immigrants into France. This has provided a new source of labor but also created some racist feeling.

As in other European countries, 1968 was a year of great political unrest in France. In France, the protest took the form of sit-ins and strikes in factories and universities, and demonstrations in the streets. Some extremists dreamed of radically

Most French people take a great interest in politics. The parliament has 577 members elected directly by the people. During elections, posters for the candidates are posted on every possible space.

changing the nature of society, although many students were merely discontented with the way the universities were run.

When the crisis was over, improved wages and conditions were granted to workers, and a university reform bill was adopted. Teachers and students were also granted a greater voice in the running of the universities. There have been some changes in French education since 1968, but not as many as were hoped for.

In recent years, France has made great steps toward modernizing the country in its own individual way. France has kept its own identity, resisting the idea of blindly adopting the life style of other western countries.

49

6 Farming the Land

Until the eighteenth century, the main crop in France was wheat. This was because the staple diet of the people was bread, and very little, if any, meat was eaten. The land was sown with wheat for two years or, in the case of the south of France, for only one year. Then, in the following year, the land was allowed to rest. This is called letting the land lie fallow. The poor vegetation that did grow on the land during the fallow year was used by the livestock to graze on.

Grass for cattle to eat was in short supply and as a result, cattle were rare. The few animals that peasants did own were used to pull farm equipment and to fertilize the soil. The animals were not killed for meat. Sheep were popular because they did not eat much and because they produced wool.

The fallow method

The peasants found it very hard to build up stocks and a bad harvest often led to famine. The fallow method was very difficult to get away from. It has been called a vicious circle, it works like this:

1 Few cattle means lack of fertilizer

 2 Land must lie fallow because of lack of fertilizer

3 Low production because only two-thirds of land is in use

 5 Only one-third of land is available for grazing land **4** All land devoted to producing crops

In many parts of France there are still very few cattle. Some farms have only one or two cows, so it is still possible to see cows being milked by hand.

The way out of this vicious circle was to sow land that was lying fallow with grass seed, thus providing enough food for cattle.

In the nineteenth century, towns grew up around industry but the people who worked in the towns needed more food. They now not only wanted wheat but meat and dairy products as well. Mechanical farming equipment was developed so that more land could be cultivated to cope with the demand.

Increasing productivity

Until the end of World War II, most farms cultivated more than one type of crop and raised livestock, too. Productivity was low. In order to increase it, farmers were encouraged to modernize their farms and to specialize in growing specific crops or in raising certain livestock. From 1960 to 1984 the number of farms in France dropped from just under 1.8 million to just over one million. This does not mean that there is less land being farmed but that farms are getting bigger. Many small farms have been added to other farms to create larger concerns. Farmers have also formed cooperatives, sharing large machinery and labor. France has 1.5 million tractors, a total of six percent of the world's tractors compared with 19 percent owned by farmers in the United States.

At the beginning of the twentieth century, France was still very much an agricultural nation with 40 percent of its population working the land. Today, only three percent of the population are farmers. However, farmland still covers more than 57 percent of the country.

Farmers work very hard and they go on vacation less than other groups of the population. Many have a lower standard of living than other French people. There are a number of different kinds of French farmers. At one end of the scale there are still farm hands who work from six in the morning until ten at night. They milk the cows and goats by hand in the fields and often sleep in one of the farm's outbuildings. At the other extreme, there are big farm owners who run their farms like modern production machines.

The plains of northern France make fertile farmland. The rolling hills stretch for mile after mile, sown with crops such as wheat and corn. The open land allows modern farming methods to be utilized.

Most French farms are very efficient. However, some of the EEC's policies, such as maintaining special prices, have encouraged farmers to produce too much. This overproduction has led to food surpluses such as "butter mountains" and "wine lakes." France is the largest producer of wine in the world, producing 7.56 million tons of wine in 1985. The French people are convinced their wine is the best in the world.

The château of Meursault is in the important wine growing region of Burgundy. The wines that are grown by each château are called château bottled. The wine from each château is different from others. Meursault is well known for its fine wine.

The French wine industry keeps a close eye on the standard of wine it produces. A good wine must meet certain requirements. When a wine is awarded the label *Appellation d'Origine Controlée*, or AOC, this means it is of guaranteed high quality.

The Main Products of Agriculture

Wine	7.56 million tons	1st in world
Wheat	32 million tons	5th in world
Sugar	4.78 million tons	7th in world
Corn	13 million tons	8th in world
Cattle	23.1 million head	10th in world
Beef and Veal	2 million tons	5th in world
Pork	1.98 million tons	5th in world
All Meats	6.06 million tons	4th in world
Milk	36.4 million tons	3rd in world after U.S.S.R and U.S.A.

7

The Economy, Industry, and Energy of France

Economy and industry

The end of World War II left France with a tattered economy. Many towns, especially in the north, had been heavily damaged by bombing. Roads, bridges, railroads, ports, and factories were destroyed. In the end, however, this destruction proved to be an advantage. France, like West Germany, was able to rebuild its economy and industry with new industrial installations and better means of communication.

Soon after the war, France decided to adopt a five-year economic plan similar to that of the Soviet Union. The first five-year plan, called Plan Monnet after its founder, stretched from 1947 to 1952. Its aim was to get France's transportation and basic industries such as coal, steel, iron, and energy back on their feet. Housing was also needed but this took second place to rebuilding industry.

Later plans included social as well as economic measures. The government made an effort to decentralize industry from the Paris region in order to provide work for people in the poorer areas of France. The modernization of agriculture was also encouraged. In 1958, trade was eased by the lowering of customs barriers between the countries of Luxembourg, Belgium, Holland, France, West Germany, and Italy. These were the six founding members of the EEC. The common market meant that competition between the member states grew. This forced France to make its industry more competitive with other EEC countries.

France's prewar traditional industry had achieved a high degree of craftsmanship, but with a low level of productivity. Now this had to change. France had to compete with five other industrialized countries in a larger market, and so needed to make and sell more. More research, better equipment, and better managing and marketing techniques were required. France's economy gradually became stronger and more competitive. Now, France is the fifth largest industrial producer in the world and is also the fifth among world exporters.

Exports

The traditional goods for which France is renowned include fine china, wine, perfume, and textiles. France now has some very successful firms producing cars, electronics, tires, and chemicals. France exports over 56 percent of its car production, making car firms like Renault, Citroën, and Peugeot household names all over the world. Michelin is well known, not only for its tires but also its maps and guide books. Oil refining is one of the most important industries, since France not only produces its own oil but also imports crude oil for refining.

Agriculture of course still plays a major part in the economy. France is the fifth producer of beef, wheat, and pork in the world and the third producer of milk in the world.

France produces several makes of cars that are sold all over the world. Car manufacture is a high technology industry and uses computers and robots whenever possible. This worker in a Renault factor is testing an engine before it is installed in a car.

Like other countries in Europe, France has an unemployment problem, and over ten percent of people of working age do not have a job.

Energy

France has many sources of energy. Coal, the most traditional source, is found mainly in northern and eastern France. Unfortunately, coal reserves are slowly running out and are becoming more expensive to extract. Large reserves of natural gas have been found at Lacq in southwestern France, but these also are likely to run out, probably by the end of the century.

France has to import most of the oil it uses, even though there are oil fields in the Landes district. However, the French are prospecting for

oil off the west coast of Brittany with some hope of success.

As a result of the lack of natural resources, France has developed a number of other ways of producing energy. Dams have been built in the Pyrenees and the Massif Central, and on the Rhône and the Rhine as well as other French rivers in the Alps. These produce hydroelectricity or "white coal," *houille blanche*, as the French call it.

Experiments have been made with various new forms of energy, including solar power, hot springs deep underground, and tidal energy. Tidal energy is produced by a dam on the Rance River near St. Malo in Brittany. The dam is 800 yards long and harnesses some of the strongest tides in the world, with the help of turbines. These work while the tide is going in and out. Unfortunately, the dam produces less than one percent of the nation's electricity needs.

Nuclear power

France has had an important nuclear power program since 1967, and by 1986 was the second producer of atomic energy in the world after the United States. Two-thirds of the country's electricity is produced by atomic energy. France now has enough nuclear energy to be able to start selling considerable amounts of nuclear-generated electricity overseas.

The Rance River rises in Brittany and flows east and north to the Gulf of St. Malo. The tides in this part of the French coast rise and fall sharply. In 1966, a barrage was built across the river to use the force of this water to create the world's first successful tidal power station.

59

8 Transportation and Communications

France's central position in western Europe means that since early history it has always been a focus for all kinds of visitors. France's transportation system, like so many areas of French life, centers on Paris which is at the heart of a network that stretches to all parts of France. The links between regions are not as good as those of each region with Paris.

Trains

The French railway of SNCF (*Société Nationale des Chemins de Fer Français*) has a reputation for being fast, efficient, and punctual. This is largely due to the fact that the SNCF was able to start from scratch after the war and create a new system with new equipment.

After 1944, the network was streamlined to make it more economical, and money was put into improving the service and developing new methods for moving passengers more efficiently. Passengers must now punch their own tickets by machine before boarding the train.

The latest in a line of new fast trains, which includes the Mistral and the Turbo trains, is the high-speed TGV or *Train à Grande Vitesse*. This train averages 133 miles per hour. New tracks were put down especially for the TGV, and the first line to be completed was the Paris-Lyon-Marseille run. This line now carries over 16 million passengers a year, taking only two hours

The French high-speed train, or TGV, waiting at Lyon Station before continuing on its journey from Marseille to Paris. This journey is now so fast, efficient, and comfortable that it rivals the airlines' service. The TGV is not a diesel engine but is powered by overhead electric cables.

to get from Paris to Lyon, a distance of 319 miles. The SNCF plans to expand the TGV network in other directions out of Paris toward the south and west.

The SNCF is widely used because of its efficiency and reliability. So much emphasis is placed on punctuality that if an engineer does not keep on time and has no real excuse, he or she is fined. This obviously finds favor with passengers, because on 287,000 miles of track the SNCF carries more than 776 million passengers a year!

Roads

Just as with the railroad network, the road system in France is centralized with many roads leading to Paris. France's roads range from superhighways (*Autoroutes*), main roads (*Routes Nationales*), and secondary roads (*Routes Départementales*) to small country roads (*Routes Communales*). France is said to have one of the most dense road networks in the world, with over 500,000 miles of roads.

To ease the overcrowded minor roads, the French have developed a superhighway system. It is now the fourth largest network after the United States, Australia, and West Germany. The 3,750 miles of highways cover all main routes and each one has a name such as *Autoroute du Soleil* or the Turnpike of the Sun. The highways have tolls, meaning that, even though they are efficient, many people avoid them in favor of the old main roads where they don't have to pay. Nevertheless, when the vacation season starts, popular roads such as the Paris-Lyon-Côte d'Azur route are jammed with cars.

A typical French country road is straight for mile after mile, well surfaced, and lined with trees. Tradition says that Napoleon ordered that trees should be planted so that his armies would always march in the shade.

People are not allowed to drive until they are 18, and the driving test is both a written and a practical exam. Younger people, however, are permitted to ride mopeds as soon as they are 14 years old and no test is required. Some young people spend a lot of time and money customizing their motor vehicles to make them unique.

The French tend to be fast drivers, with little patience. Although the use of the car horn is illegal in built-up areas, this never deters the French from giving vent to their feelings in traffic jams by honking their horns. When a wedding car goes by, it is customary to honk at the bride to wish her luck. On December 31 people will also honk in the New Year on the Champs Elysées in Paris, a noise that must be heard to be believed!

This is a typical view of a "D" class road in the south of France. The road is very straight and lined on each side by plane trees, which shade the travelers from the very hot sun. Farther north, the trees are usually the Lombardy poplar.

Public transportation in Paris is very popular and has been called "every household's second car." In Paris, buses carry as many passengers in a year as all the French railroads do. In rural areas where trains no longer run, buses are used.

Air

France has three airlines. Air Inter deals with internal flights which represent over a third of all flights. UTA specializes in long-distance flights to the Far East and French overseas territories. Air France is the main airline which handles international flights. The most popular international route is between France and Britain, carrying about four million passengers annually. France has many regional airports but the principal airports are in Paris. The Paris airport group is the second largest in Europe, after London. There are three airports: Le Bourget which was the first to be built, Orly, and Roissy-Charles de Gaulle, the largest, opened in the mid-1970s.

At Charles de Gaulle airport, the futuristic design of the terminals has people going up and down plexiglass tubes on conveyor belts to various "satellite terminals" from which they board their planes.

France's biggest aircraft company is called Aérospatiale. Since the war, Aérospatiale has developed many new planes that have helped to put France's aircraft industry back on its feet. The Caravelle which first flew in 1959, and the Airbus, which made its debut in 1974, have both done well.

Aérospatiale's most well known creation has been Concorde, which was developed in cooperation with Britain. Concorde has shattered the time it once took a passenger flight to cross the Atlantic. Flying at 1,118 miles per hour, Concorde takes less than three and a half hours to get from Paris to New York, whereas an ordinary flight takes twice this time.

Marseille, in the south, is France's most important seaport. It has a large harbor in the Golfe du Lion which is used by the French navy, oil tankers, and other large freighters. With a population of nearly one million, Marseille is also a center for commerce and industry.

Water

France's 4,971 miles of waterways are concentrated in the northeastern part of the country. There are 3,107 miles of canals and 1,864 miles of rivers, which are mostly used to transport heavy goods such as coal and iron on barges. About eight percent of all French goods are carried on the canals and seven percent through pipelines. France has never really been a major seafaring nation like Britain or Holland and today it is ranked eighteenth in the world, with a merchant fleet of 924 vessels. France's principal seaports are Le Havre in the north for the Atlantic traffic and Marseille in the south for the Mediterranean Sea.

New engineering developments

France is always eager both to start and to develop new engineering techniques. Since the war many projects have been completed to aid transportation and communications. In 1964, the Mont Blanc tunnel in the French Alps was opened, linking France to northern Italy. The Tancarville suspension bridge over the Seine estuary, near Le Havre in Normandy, has saved long detours previously needed to cross the river.

Recently, France and Britain have started on an ambitious project to link both countries by tunnel. Two attempts were made during the last century to do this, so the idea is not new. When completed in 1993, the 32-mile-long tunnel will joint Folkestone, in the south of England, to Sangatte, near Calais in the north of France. The "Chunnel" will be the longest undersea tunnel in the world. According to estimates, over 7.5 million tons of rubble will have to be removed as it is being dug. When completed, the tunnel will contain three smaller tunnels. Two of these will be for railroad tracks and the other will be a service tunnel. Single- and double-decker trains, called shuttles, will transport cars and trucks in 30 minutes from Folkestone to Sangatte. A train from Paris to London will take only three hours!

Telephones

Nowadays 89 percent of French households have a phone. The service has improved greatly over the years. The average wait of 11 months in 1975 to get a telephone installed is now only two or three weeks.

Technically the telephone has also improved.

This girl is using a Minitel, which is like an electronic telephone directory. It can be used to find out other information and there are many Minitels in banks, post offices, and other public places, and also in people's homes.

Most phone exchanges are now automatic, and many more lines have been installed. In ten years, the number of main lines has tripled, and there are now over 20.8 million.

An exciting new development is the Minitel or electronic telephone directory. There are now over 1.3 million Minitels in France. Phones are linked to a bank of information that not only includes phone numbers, but also timetables for air, rail, and road travel, weather information, theater and concert programs, sports results, horoscopes, and much more. When you use the Minitel directory service, the first three minutes are free.

The post office
French people send about 15 billion letters a year. There are over 21,000 post offices in France to deal with all this mail. The French post office is known as the PTT or *Poste Télégraphe Téléphone*. The post office's symbol is the swallow, and the post boxes and vans are yellow. The PTT performs many services apart from sending letters and dealing with phone calls. It also offers banking services and hands out pension checks. In many small villages the post office is a lifeline to the world, even though it is open only a few hours a day.

Television and radio
It is estimated that French people spend about a fifth of their time watching television or listening to the radio. France has its own television system called SECAM with six channels: TF1, A2, FR3, Canal+, La Cinq, and M6. All channels show advertisements and are independently owned except for A2, which is partly state run. To receive Canal+ viewers must rent an electronic box to decode signals. Besides these main channels there are also cable and satellite channels. People in some parts of France can watch as many as 20 different television channels.

French television has also always shown a lot of feature films, both French and foreign. Arts programs discuss the latest films and directors, giving them the same importance as other visual arts. Today there are many American and British series and films shown in France. Television is gradually losing its typically French identity.

The French have a variety of radio stations. France Musique plays classical music. France

News and magazines are popular in France and, in a large city, a wide range of national papers and even foreign papers, such as the Herald Tribune, *may be sold.* Le Monde *and* Le Figaro *are the most renowned French papers.*

Culture broadcasts discussions, plays, and cultural programs. Europe Numero Un and RTL have a variety of games and quiz programs, phone-ins, and pop music. France has a telecommunications station at Pleumeur-Boudou in Brittany which picks up signals from satellites that are in orbit above the earth.

Newspapers

Over 80 newspapers are printed every day in France. Most daily papers come out the evening before. There are various regional papers, such as *Ouest-France* that caters to Normandy and Brittany. The principal daily papers are *Le Monde, Le Figaro, France-Soir, Le Matin, Liberation,* and *Le Canard Enchainé.*

9 The People and Their Way of Life

There is no such thing as a typical French person. There is, however, a French way of life: that is, how the French are educated, what they believe, what they eat and drink, where they go on vacation, and what they do with their spare time.

Over the centuries France has undergone many wars, invasions, and occupations. Franks, Romans, Normans, Celts, Visigoths, and Burgundians have stayed to settle in what is now France. The French nation is thus a complex mixture of many races and civilizations.

More recently people from old French colonies in north and western Africa, as well as from other parts of the world, have immigrated to France. This has added a new wave of population.

Where the French live
Many French people live in apartments which come in all shapes, sizes, and ages. These homes range from large luxury apartments to HLM apartments (*Habitation à Loyer Modérée*) which are public housing apartments for families with low incomes. Some of the older apartments are very beautiful, with high ceilings, parquet floors, elaborate fireplaces, and servants' quarters on the top floor. Apartment buildings are very popular, especially in Paris. In new towns there are gigantic modern apartment buildings.

People living in the country or on the outskirts of populated areas often live in houses. The style of houses varies throughout the country.

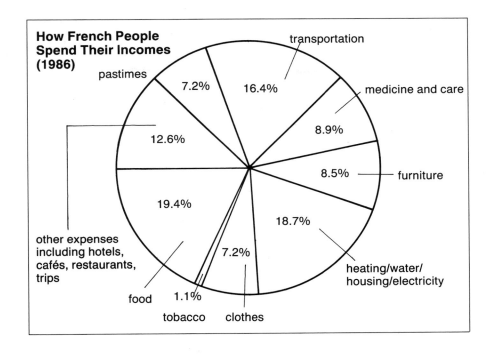

How French People Spend Their Incomes (1986)

- pastimes — 7.2%
- transportation — 16.4%
- medicine and care — 8.9%
- furniture — 8.5%
- 12.6%
- 19.4%
- 18.7% — heating/water/housing/electricity
- other expenses including hotels, cafés, restaurants, trips
- food
- tobacco — 1.1%
- clothes — 7.2%

Language

The national language of France is French. It is also spoken in Belgium, Luxembourg, and Switzerland as well as many old French colonies such as Algeria, Tunisia, Morocco, Quebec in Canada, western and central Africa, and Vietnam. French was once the language used by diplomats all over the world. The French spoken today bears little resemblance to the Celtic language, once spoken in what is now France. The many invasions France has undergone have influenced and molded today's rich and musical language. Latin, Persian, Arabic, and Germanic dialects as well as traces of regional dialects are all evident.

Most French people live in apartments. Sometimes these apartments are in large new buildings and sometimes they are in older buildings like these in Nice, which are only six or seven stories high.

Recently, English words have crept into the French language. These new words are often sports-related or words for which French has no equivalent. French people who use too many English words are sometimes accused of speaking *Franglais*.

Auxerre in the Bourgogne region is similar to many other French towns, with its beautiful churches, tree-lined streets, squares, and historic buildings. The older area is bordered by a thriving new town of factories, offices, and residential area that are typical of modern France.

Here Are a Few English Words the French Use

un short	un sweatshirt
stop	le marketing
le weekend	le shopping
un pullover	checkup
un sandwich	un checklist
le football	un snob
le basket (basketball)	un snack bar
le tennis	un drug store
le toast	le fast-food
la marmalade	un clown
le parking (lot)	un club
une penalty	un cocktail
un corner	un cockpit
un skateboard	le pudding
le chewing gum	le cake
un cardigan	cool
le breakfast	

However, French has also influenced English very strongly. Today's English language is a mixture of many different ancient languages including Norman French. This dates back to the invasion of William the Conqueror in 1066 when French was spoken by the nobility. There are some interesting differences. The English words used for meat come from the French as in:

beef	pork	mutton
boeuf	*porc*	*mouton*

This is because the Norman rulers referred to meat with these words at the dining table. The words for the animals themselves, such as cow, pig, or sheep, come from old English. This is because the English peasants tended the animals.

73

Some French Words Used in English		
café	cliché	cul-de-sac
restaurant	hors d'oeuvres	chef
entrée	pâté	menu
quiche	éclair	croissant
buffet	nougat	mousse
béret	soufflé	role
discothèque	crochet	chic
boutique	fiancé (and fiancée)	rendezvous

Religion

The predominant religion in France is Roman Catholicism. Catholicism was an important part of French life until quite recently. In the Middle Ages, churches and great cathedrals were built throughout France, which has given the country a heritage of many beautiful buildings.

Up to 1905, the state paid clergymen's salaries, but nowadays the clergy depend on donations and collections for their income. Although many French people still consider themselves Catholics they are not practicing Catholics. Actually the number of regular churchgoers is quite low, amounting to as few as one person in ten or less. Over 90 percent of the French people are baptized and many even receive their first communion, but will rarely been seen at Mass after that date except on special occasions. The Church is not very popular with the younger generation.

As well as dwindling congregations fewer people are now entering the priesthood. Where there was once a priest for each parish, there is now sometimes only one to cover as many as six parishes.

France also has a small minority of Protestants

Processions through the streets are a common sight in France. They take place on various religious festivals and are often used as an occasion for children to make their first communion. The communicants always dress in white, which symbolizes their innocence and purity.

which amounts to only three percent of the population. Other religions, such as Islam, are now also practiced by immigrants from North Africa.

Education

Most French children begin their school lives at nursery school. Some children even start school as young as two years old. Compulsory education, however, starts at the age of six. The first grade a pupil enters is the 12th grade, *la douzième,* followed by the 11th and so on, because French grades are numbered in reverse order.

A typical elementary school day might start at 8:30 a.m. and finish at 4:30 p.m. with two hours off for lunch. Children go to school on Saturday mornings as well, but Wednesday school is closed. On Wednesday, many children go to the local youth center, the Maison des Jeunes et de la Culture, where they can join classes and enjoy sports activities. Wednesday is also the day when religious classes, similar to Sunday school classes, are held at local churches.

Secondary schools
When they are 11 years old, children move to high school which is the Collège d'Enseignement Secondaire, or CES. At the CES children study for four years, from the sixth grade to the third. The school day is longer than at elementary school, and may sometimes start as early as 8 a.m. and finish at 5 p.m. French school children have a long lunch break, sometimes as long as two hours. The school meals are generally popular with pupils. A sample menu is shown on the right.

As with elementary schools, many high schools have classes on Saturday mornings, although some now open on Wednesday mornings instead. Pupils study a wide range of subjects including modern languages, crafts, and technical drawing, as well as sciences, history, and mathematics.

At the end of the fifth grade, when they are 13 years-old, pupils are offered a number of choices.

A Typical School Lunch Menu

Lundi	carottes oeuf dur	Monday	grated carrots and boiled egg
	lapin purée		rabbit and mashed potatoes
	Camembert		cheese
Mardi	salade composée	Tuesday	mixed salad
	côte de porc		pork chop
	choux de bruxelles		brussels sprouts
	banane		banana
Mercredi	saucission	Wednesday	spicy sausage
	paupiettes de veau		stuffed veal rolls
	petits pois, carottes		peas and carrots
	orange		orange
Jeudi	salades de tomates	Thursday	tomato salad
	bifteck		steak
	frites		french fries
	fruit		fruit
Vendredi	betraves concombre	Friday	cucumber and beets
	poisson pané		breaded fish
	frites		french fries
	pomme		apple

Students may continue to receive a general education, they may go on to study in a Lycée Technique, or technical school. A further choice is to follow an apprenticeship in a particular trade.

Standards of work at school are high. Students are expected to maintain a good grade average. If teachers and parents are not satisfied with the level of work, a pupil may have to repeat a year.

Pupils must provide all their own textbooks,

paper, workbooks, files, and other materials. Schools rarely have lockers for pupils so books have to be brought to school each day in the student's bookbag.

The Baccalauréat

At the end of the third grade at CES, when they are 15 years old, all pupils take an exam called *le Brevet des Collèges*. Following this exam, some choose to go to technical schools while others may decide to go the the *lycée* to prepare for their final exam. The final exam is taken when they are 18 years old and is called the Baccalauréat.

Pupils prepare for the final exam for two years, and the work load is heavy. Philosophy, French literature and language, two or three foreign languages, mathematics, history, geography, and the sciences must all be studied. There are various types of finals, each one covering the same basic subjects but with a different emphasis. The economics final, for example, places a particular emphasis on economics, history, and geography. The literary Baccalauréat, on the other hand emphasizes philosophy, French, and foreign languages.

The exam itself is marked according to a point system. The mark is compiled according to how important the subject is in the major the student has chosen.

The total marks are then added up and if the total is over 50 percent then the student has passed. The student can get a pass (*passable*), a satisfactory pass (*assez bien*), a good pass (*bien*), or a very good pass (*trés bien*).

There is a lot of prestige attached to becoming a

bachelier or Baccalauréat holder. The Baccalauréat means that a pupil can go on to higher education and should guarantee a place at a university. Those students who do go to a university tend to go to one nearby, and live at home with their parents while they study. Only one-fifth of the population in France has a Baccalauréat.

The brightest pupils will try to get a place at one of the distinguished universities, or *grandes écoles,* such as the Ecole Polytechnique. A graduate from one of the *écoles* has very good job prospects and often goes to work for the government, or one of the public services, or industry.

Vacations

French schoolchildren have two-and-a-half months' vacation in the summer. Some children are sent away to a summer camp. These are like American camps, and are located all over France. The children are supervised by young counselors who look after them and organize games and activities. The camps developed especially for children whose parents cannot afford family vacations attract over a million children every year. August is the most popular time to go on vacation and over 80 percent are taken then. The roads out of Paris are jammed with traffic at the beginning and end of vacation time, leaving Paris like a ghost city. Shops, cafés, and bakeries shut for their annual vacation.

France has such varied countryside that there is little need for the French to venture outside its borders merely for a change of scenery. On weekends, people who live in cities and towns often feel the need to get away. Some people have country homes, and others may go to visit parents and relatives who live in the country. People relax and enjoy doing odd jobs, known as *bricolage*, which is a favorite French pastime. Nearly 80 percent of those on vacation spend their time in France. For those who do go abroad, the most popular countries are Spain, Portugal, and Andorra—between France and Spain.

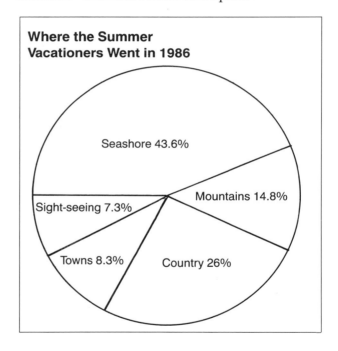

Where the Summer Vacationers Went in 1986

Seashore 43.6%

Mountains 14.8%

Sight-seeing 7.3%

Towns 8.3%

Country 26%

Other vacations

French people often go for skiing vacations in the winter, especially during the February school recess. The majority of vacationers go to the ski resorts in the French Alps, although a number go to Italy, Austria, or Switzerland.

As the climate in France is generally good in the summer, many festivals take place outdoors. This street dance is part of the celebrations held on Bastille Day, which is July 14.

French people get up to ten holidays a year, including Christmas and Easter. Each one is celebrated in a different way.

On Labor Day, May 1, the French give one another sprigs of lily of the valley, that is meant to bring good luck. The national holiday is July 14, celebrating the storming of the Bastille and the beginning of the Revolution. There is a great military parade of troops, tanks, and guns down the Champs Elysées in Paris. Throughout France, in the evening, fireworks go off, and people dance and sing to bands in village squares late into the night.

All Saints Day or *Toussaint* is on November 1, when many French families go to place flowers on the graves of their relatives. The most popular flowers used are chrysanthemums. Armistice Day on November 11 commemorates the end of the World Wars I and II. The president places a wreath on the tomb of the unknown soldier under the Arc de Triomphe in Paris.

10 Food and Drink

French people value and appreciate food and drink. A meal is more than mere nourishment, it is a pleasure to be lingered over. Food and drink are a way of life in France.

Breakfast usually consists of coffee or hot chocolate, and a croissant or bread. A *biscotte* of dried toast may be eaten if there is no fresh bread in the house. The French put butter or jam on their bread only at breakfast. The jam is often apricot, although some people now eat marmalade. This is followed at noontime by lunch, which is the most important meal of the day. The earliest dinner is eaten at 7:30 p.m.

A typical meal includes an appetizer, a main course, cheese, dessert, coffee. Bread is always on the table but is rarely eaten with butter, except in dairy regions such as Normandy.

Popular appetizers include pâté or small slices of raw mixed vegetables called *crudités*. The most common main dish is probably steak and fried potatoes, although France has a long tradition of elaborate cooking, or *haute cuisine*, as well as its own distinctive regional dishes. Famous dishes include such delicacies as tripes à la mode de Caen from Normandy (tripe cooked in Calvados, an apple brandy), choucroute from Alsace (pickled cabbage, pork sausages, and potatoes), cassoulet from the Languedoc (French baked beans), and bouillabaise from Marseille (fish soup).

Cheese is a very important part of the meal; there are over 250 different kinds. The most common are Camembert and Pont l'Evéque from

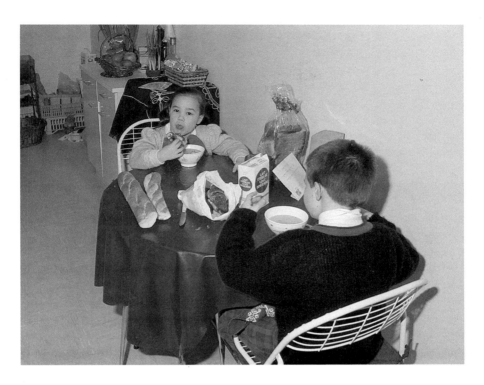

Breakfast in France is a simple meal of fresh bread or, for a treat, buttery pastries such as croissant *or* pain chocolat. *Children usually drink hot chocolate. This is served in bowls into which they dip their bread. Adults are more likely to drink large cups of coffee.*

Normandy, Roquefort, a blue cheese from the Aveyron in the south of France, Brie from east of Paris, and various goats' cheeses from all over the country. Dessert may be a piece of fruit tart or a créme caramel.

In France, wine is a natural partner to food, and it is unusual *not* to offer wine with a meal in France. In a recent year each French person consumed on average 156 pints of wine during the course of the year! This may seem to be a lot of wine but is, in fact, much less than it has been in the past. For special occasions a host will choose a different wine for every course of the meal.

Eating is a national pastime and there are excellent restaurants and cafés to be found everywhere. Whenever possible, food is eaten outside. The midday break in France is usually two hours so that lunch can be eaten in comfort.

Mineral water is often served with the meal rather than tap water, and children are allowed to drink watered down wine.

The Average Consumption of Some Foods by a French Person in a Year

Bread:	148 pounds
Wine:	156 pints
Beer:	84 pints
Cider:	34 pints
Butter:	22 pounds
Coffee and tea:	9 pounds
Potatoes:	142 pounds
Beef:	42 pounds
Cheese:	44 pounds
Sugar:	26 pounds

Table manners and customs

★ French people do not put their hands in their laps at table, they rest their hands on the table. This custom originated from the need in former times to demonstrate that you were unarmed!

★ Table napkins are important. The French place napkins on their laps slightly unfolded or, sometimes, tie them around their necks.

★ There are generally no bread plates in French restaurants—bread is simply placed by the plate.

★ Wine is always poured into the host's glass first so that the wine may be tasted to ensure that it is satisfactory. This is also done to make sure that any pieces of cork fall into the host's glass rather than in those of the guests.

★ At home and in some restaurants, people keep the same knives and forks for the first and second course.

★ Before starting a meal it is polite to say *"Bon appetit."*

★ Cheese is served before dessert not after, and is eaten with bread. A separate wine can be chosen for the dessert course.

A Café Might Serve:
Un diablo menthe: lemonade and mint syrup
Un noir: black coffee
Un crème: white coffee
Un chocolat: hot chocolate
Une pression: beer
Un pastis: anisette drink served with iced water
Un citron pressé: fresh lemon juice served with water and sugar
Un panaché: beer and lemonade
Un kir: dry white wine and black currant liqueur
Un ballon de rouge: a glass of red wine

Cafés

Cafés are a very important part of French life. A café is not just somewhere to have a drink, it is a meeting place as well. In the summer tables and chairs are put out on the sidewalk and people sit and chat and watch others go by.

Café tabacs are the only places where you can buy cigarettes in France. They are recognizable by the red cigar shaped sign outside. If there is also a Paris Mutuel Urbain or PMU sign outside, you can bet on horse races there as well as buy your lotto tickets. Lotto is a very popular national lottery game; the results are drawn live on television.

Most cafés open early in the morning, some as early as 7 a.m., and people will stop in on the way to work, for breakfast. Breakfast consists of a

Charles de Gaulle, when he was President of France, said, ''How can you be expected to govern a country that has 246 kinds of cheese.'' This is just a small example of the range of French cheeses that may be found in a good cheese shop.

croissant that is often dipped in coffee. At lunchtime some cafés serve light snacks such as sandwiches, quiches Lorraine, and so on. Another popular snack is boiled eggs which you will often find in racks on the bar. Cafés may close at any time from 8 p.m. to the early hours.

Shopping

Many French people will buy food every day from the local shops or market to ensure that the food is fresh and at its best. Frozen foods are not as widely used as in the United States or Britain although their popularity is spreading.

The average French family spends nearly 20 percent of its income on food. Shops can open for business as early as 7:30 a.m. In big cities like Paris, shops stay open all day and close at 7 or 8 p.m. In smaller towns and villages, however, shops may stay closed from noon to 4 p.m., such is the importance of lunchtime! The late closing time means that people can shop on their way home from work.

11   The Arts and Sports

Literature, the theater, painting, and films play an important part in French culture. The arts have a long tradition of brilliant writers, playwrights, and painters, of whom the French are justly proud.

Literature
France has produced world famous writers in every age. In the eighteenth century, writer-philosophers such as Diderot, Voltaire, Montesquieu, Rousseau, and many others wrote the first encyclopedia, between 1751 and 1772.

The Musée d'Orsay used to be a train station, but it has been converted into an art gallery and museum. The original design of the station can be seen in the arched glass roof. The gallery is very popular and houses an important collection of works of the Impressionist movement.

Other famous French writers include Honoré de Balzac who lived from 1799 to 1850. In his 91 novels, Balzac described in great detail the society of his day. Alexandre Dumas wrote the amazing adventures of the three musketeers and the Count of Monte Cristo. Victor Hugo, who lived from 1802 to 1885, immortalized the bell ringer of Notre Dame cathedral, in *The Hunchback of Notre Dame*. Hugo also wrote *Les Misérables*.

One novelist who greatly influenced twentieth-century writers was Marcel Proust. His major work was *In Remembrance of Things Past*, an extremely long novel based on Proust's life and experiences.

Twentieth-century writers include André Gide, André Malraux, Simone de Beauvoir, Nathalie Sarraute, Jean-Paul Sartre, and Albert Camus. Camus received the Nobel Prize for Literature in 1957.

The theater

France boasts many famous playwrights such as the seventeenth-century Pierre Corneille, Jean Racine, and of course Molière. Molière is perhaps the most famous and popular of French dramatists.

In his plays, Molière criticized the society of the day. Incompetent doctors, arranged marriages, snobs, pretentious women, and religious hypocrisy are all among his subjects. His most famous plays include *The Bourgeois Gentilhomme, Tartuffe,* and *Le Malade Imaginaire*. Molière died on stage in 1673.

Other famous French playwrights include Jean Anouilh, Jean Giraudoux, Jean Genet, and Eugene Ionesco.

Paintings

Painting is much appreciated in France. Influential French painters of the seventeenth century include Georges de la Tour, Nicolas Poussin, and Jean Antoine Watteau.

Jacques Louis David was an eighteenth-century painter who was popular with both the revolutionaries and Napoleon. He painted such well-known masterpieces as *The Death of Marat* and *The Coronation of Napoleon*. Other eighteenth-century painters were Théodore Géricault and Eugène Delacroix.

Perhaps the most famous French painters are the Impressionists. Impressionist painters such as Manet, Monet, Corot, Pissarro, and Renoir revolutionized the painting techniques of the day. The Impressionists applied paint in dabs and dashes using many different colors and created an effect of light and shade.

Signac and Seurat carried the Impressionists' technique into points and dots or *pointillism*. Painters who came after the Impressionists were called Post-Impressionists, and included Edgar Degas, Henri de Toulouse-Laútrec, Paul Gauguin, and Vincent Van Gogh.

Other painters of note are Henri Matisse, Paul Cézanne, who influenced the later abstract artists, and Georges Braque, the cubist painter.

Music

Some of the world's greatest composers have been French, including Fauré, Couperin, Berlioz, Debussy, Bizet, and Offenbach. Bizet created the much loved opera *Carmen*. Debussy was inspired by poets such as Verlaine, Mallarmé, and Edgar

Allan Poe. Debussy was also interested in the Impressionist movement.

The French people not only have a great heritage of classical music but one of popular music as well. Maurice Chevalier toured the world as an entertainer and Edith Piaf sang songs such as *Je ne regrette rien* and *La vie en rose* which have become legendary.

Charles Aznavour, Sacha Distel, and Jean-Michel Jarre are other well known French artists.

Cinema

Filmmaking is held in such esteem in France that it is known as "the Seventh Art." One of the earliest films, presented in 1895, was made by two French brothers, the Lumières.

One of the greatest of the early French filmmakers is considered to be Jean Renoir, the son of Auguste Renoir the Impressionist painter. He was born in 1894. Later directors included François Truffaut, Jean-Luc Godard (both from the 1950s New Wave of cinema), Claude Chabrol, Louis Malle, and Michel Deville.

Sports and leisure

Sports are a growing part of French life. There are over 60 different sports associations in France and over 100,000 sports clubs. New sports complexes are being built throughout the country.

Young people get physical education lessons at school and on Wednesday afternoons they also enjoy all kinds of sports at the local Association Sportive or AS. There are many different sports practiced in France; the most popular is soccer. France has always had an interest in sports of all

The Tour de France is a bicycle road race that is very popular. It is taken in 20 stages and lasts about three weeks. As the contestants pass through the different towns, there is always a crowd to cheer them on. The race starts in a different town each year but always ends in Paris.

kinds. It is thanks to a Frenchman that the modern Olympic Games came into existence, organized by Baron Pierre de Coubertin, in 1896.

The world's most famous cycling race is the Tour de France, first held in 1903. The cyclists cover over 3,000 miles of arduous mountain passes, sweltering southern roads, and bumpy cobblestone streets. The first stoneroad race in France was held in 1895, from Paris to Bordeaux. Other well known automobile race car events are the Monte Carlo Rally, first held in 1911, and the Paris-Dakar which starts on New Year's Day from Paris. Perhaps most famous of all is the 24-hour Le Mans race. It is the oldest race to take place on the circuit on which it started.

Tennis is also very popular in France. The Roland Garros tennis tournament is held near Paris every year. It ranks as one of the world's four top tennis tournaments.

The mountains of France are ideal places for skiing. Many school groups throughout France go to the mountains to enjoy skiing for a whole month.

Other important sports include Rugby football, which is very popular in the south, fencing, fishing, hunting, and horse racing. The most famous French horse race is the Prix de l'Arc de Triomphe, held every year in October at Long-champs near Paris.

Traditional games

As well as practicing a wide range of modern sports, the French also play traditional games such as pelota (jai alai) and boules.

Boules is perhaps the most widespread and typically French game. It is a form of outdoor bowling. There is no need for a special green or field, however. As long as the ground is flat boules can be played anywhere. Groups of people can often be seen playing in parks, by the side of the road, or in village squares opposite the café.

Boules is played all over France and is taken very seriously.

Index